German - Greek

Teach Your Child to Read

700 Short Easy Sentences

Name 

I Can...

- [ ] read the 1st sentence.
- [ ] read the 2nd sentence.
- [ ] read the 3rd sentence.
- [ ] make my own sentence.
- [ ] color a picture.

Der Frosch geht auf eine Party.

Ο βάτραχος πηγαίνει σε πάρτι.

The frog is going to a party.

Der grüne Frosch trägt einen grünen Hut.

Ο πράσινος βάτραχος φοράει πράσινο καπέλο.

The green frog is wearing a green hat.

Name

I Can...

- [ ] read the 1st sentence.
- [ ] read the 2nd sentence.
- [ ] read the 3rd sentence.
- [ ] make my own sentence.
- [ ] color a picture.

Eule liest gern große Bücher.

Η κουκουβάγια αρέσει να διαβάζει μεγάλα βιβλία.

Owl likes to read big books.

Die junge braune Eule lernt lesen.

Η νεαρή καφέ κουκουβάγια μαθαίνει να διαβάζει.

The young brown owl is learning to read.

Name

I Can...

- [ ] read the 1st sentence.
- [ ] read the 2nd sentence.
- [ ] read the 3rd sentence.
- [ ] make my own sentence.
- [ ] color a picture.

Komm schon! Der Eiswagen ist da!

Έλα! Το παγωτό φορτηγό είναι εδώ!

Come on! The ice cream truck is here!

Der Eiswagen spielt ein schönes Lied.

Το παγωτό φορτηγό παίζει ένα όμορφο τραγούδι.

The ice cream truck is playing a beautiful song.

Name

I Can...

- ☐ read the 1st sentence.
- ☐ read the 2nd sentence.
- ☐ read the 3rd sentence.
- ☐ make my own sentence.
- ☐ color a picture.

Drachen sind sehr freundlich und haben Schuppen auf dem Rücken.

Οι δράκοι είναι πολύ φιλικοί και έχουν κλίμακες στις πλάτες τους.

Dragons are very friendly and have scales on their backs.

Der große antike Drache sagt Hallo zu dir.

Ο μεγάλος αρχαίος δράκος σας λέει γεια σας.

The big ancient dragon says hello to you.

Name

I Can...

- [ ] read the 1st sentence.
- [ ] read the 2nd sentence.
- [ ] read the 3rd sentence.
- [ ] make my own sentence.
- [ ] color a picture.

Dieser Widder wohnt im Bauernhaus.

Αυτός ο κριός ζει στην αγροικία.

This ram lives in the farmhouse.

Der Widder lächelt, weil er gerade gebadet hat.

Ο κριός χαμογελάει επειδή πήρε λίγο μπάνιο.

The ram is smiling because it just took a bath.

I Can...

- [ ] read the 1st sentence.
- [ ] read the 2nd sentence.
- [ ] read the 3rd sentence.
- [ ] make my own sentence.
- [ ] color a picture.

Der Hase isst gerne Karotten.

Το λαγουδάκι αρέσει να τρώει καρότα.

The bunny likes to eat carrots.

Der Hase bringt seiner Familie eine Riesenmöhre zum Abendessen.

Το λαγουδάκι φέρνει ένα γίγαντα καρότο στην οικογένειά του για δείπνο.

The bunny is bringing a giant carrot to its family for dinner.

Name

I Can...

- [ ] read the 1st sentence.
- [ ] read the 2nd sentence.
- [ ] read the 3rd sentence.
- [ ] make my own sentence.
- [ ] color a picture.

Der Clown verschenkt gern Luftballons an kleine Kinder.

Ο κλόουν θέλει να δώσει μπαλόνια σε μικρά παιδιά.

The clown likes to give out balloons to little kids.

Der Clown hält drei bunte Luftballons.

Ο κλόουν κρατάει τρία πολύχρωμα μπαλόνια.

The clown is holding three colorful balloons.

Name _______________________ 

I Can...

- [ ] read the 1st sentence.
- [ ] read the 2nd sentence.
- [ ] read the 3rd sentence.
- [ ] make my own sentence.
- [ ] color a picture.

Der Clown jongliert Bälle für seine Leistung.

Ο κλόουν ζυγίζει μπάλες για την απόδοσή του.

The clown is juggling balls for his performance.

Der lustige Clown jongliert mit Geschicklichkeit.

Ο αστεία κλόουν ζευγαρώνει με επιδεξιότητα.

The funny clown is juggling with skill.

Name _________________________ 

I Can...

- [ ] read the 1st sentence.
- [ ] read the 2nd sentence.
- [ ] read the 3rd sentence.
- [ ] make my own sentence.
- [ ] color a picture.

Der Osterhase wird Schokoladeneier ausgeben.

Το Πάσχα Μπάνι πρόκειται να δώσει τα αυγά σοκολάτας.

The Easter Bunny is going to give out chocolate eggs.

Das Kaninchen pflückte gerade ein paar Karotten aus dem Garten.

Το κουνέλι απλώς έκοψε μερικά καρότα έξω από τον κήπο.

The rabbit just plucked some carrots out of the garden.

Name

I Can...

- [ ] read the 1st sentence.
- [ ] read the 2nd sentence.
- [ ] read the 3rd sentence.
- [ ] make my own sentence.
- [ ] color a picture.

Der Bleistift zeichnet eine Zick-Zack-Linie.

Το μολύβι σχεδιάζει μια γραμμή ζιγκ-ζαγκ.

The pencil is drawing a zig-zag line.

Der Bleistift kritzelt eine Linie mit der Mine.

Το μολύβι γράφει μια γραμμή με το μόλυβδο.

The pencil is scribbling a line with the lead.

Name

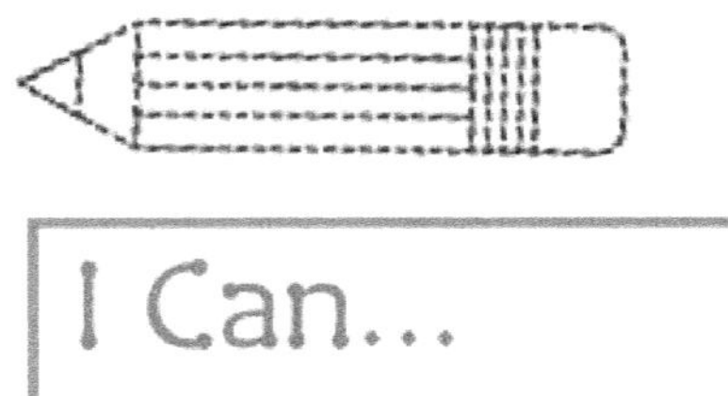

I Can...

- [ ] read the 1st sentence.
- [ ] read the 2nd sentence.
- [ ] read the 3rd sentence.
- [ ] make my own sentence.
- [ ] color a picture.

Der Bleistift setzte ein breites Lächeln auf und machte sich an die Arbeit.

Το μολύβι έβαλε ένα μεγάλο χαμόγελο και πήγε στη δουλειά.

The pencil put on a big smile and went to work.

Der Stift wacht hell und früh auf, um zur Arbeit zu gehen.

Το μολύβι ξυπνάει φωτεινό και νωρίς για να πάει στη δουλειά.

The pencil wakes up bright and early to go to work.

Name

I Can...

- [ ] read the 1st sentence.
- [ ] read the 2nd sentence.
- [ ] read the 3rd sentence.
- [ ] make my own sentence.
- [ ] color a picture.

Dieser Schneemann ist mein Freund und er ist ein Helfer des Weihnachtsmanns.

Αυτός ο χιονάνθρωπος είναι ο φίλος μου και είναι βοηθός του Σάντα.

This snowman is my friend, and he is a helper of Santa.

Der Schneemann feiert Weihnachten.

Ο χιονάνθρωπος έχει ένα χριστουγεννιάτικο πάρτι.

The snowman is having a Christmas party.

Name ____________________

I Can...

- [ ] read the 1st sentence.
- [ ] read the 2nd sentence.
- [ ] read the 3rd sentence.
- [ ] make my own sentence.
- [ ] color a picture.

Die Krake arbeitet als Koch und serviert Essen.

Το χταπόδι δουλεύει ως σεφ και σερβίρει φαγητό.

The octopus is working as a chef and serving food.

Der Tintenfisch kochte köstliches Essen für seine Freunde.

Το χταπόδι μαγειρεμένο νόστιμο φαγητό για τους φίλους του.

The octopus cooked delicious food for its friends.

Name

I Can...

- ☐ read the 1st sentence.
- ☐ read the 2nd sentence.
- ☐ read the 3rd sentence.
- ☐ make my own sentence.
- ☐ color a picture.

Der Weihnachtsmann ist glücklich.

Ο Σάντα είναι χαρούμενος.

Santa is happy.

Der Weihnachtsmann liefert den Kindern Geschenke.

Ο Άγιος Βασίλης δίνει δώρα στα παιδιά.

Santa Claus is delivering presents to the children.

Name 

I Can...

- [ ] read the 1st sentence.
- [ ] read the 2nd sentence.
- [ ] read the 3rd sentence.
- [ ] make my own sentence.
- [ ] color a picture.

Der Bär isst gerne Süßigkeiten.

Η αρκούδα αρέσει να τρώει γλυκά.

The bear likes to eat sweets.

Der braune Teddybär trägt einen hellgrünen Hut.

Το καφέ αρκουδάκι φοράει ένα φωτεινό πράσινο καπέλο.

The brown teddy bear is wearing a bright green hat.

Name _______________

I Can...

- [ ] read the 1st sentence.
- [ ] read the 2nd sentence.
- [ ] read the 3rd sentence.
- [ ] make my own sentence.
- [ ] color a picture.

Das Buch hat einen Zauberstab.

Το βιβλίο έχει μια ραβδί.

The book has a wand.

Der Junge bekam zu seinem Geburtstag eine Zauberer-Actionfigur.

Το αγόρι πήρε έναν αριθμητή δράσης για τα γενέθλιά του.

The boy got a wizard action figure for his birthday.

Name ____________________

I Can...

- [ ] read the 1st sentence.
- [ ] read the 2nd sentence.
- [ ] read the 3rd sentence.
- [ ] make my own sentence.
- [ ] color a picture.

Der Bär hat ein Geschenk.

Η αρκούδα έχει ένα δώρο.

The bear has a present.

Der Teddybär öffnet sein zweites Geschenk.

Το αρκουδάκι ανοίγει το δεύτερο του δώρο.

The teddy bear is opening his second present.

Name 

I Can...

- [ ] read the 1st sentence.
- [ ] read the 2nd sentence.
- [ ] read the 3rd sentence.
- [ ] make my own sentence.
- [ ] color a picture.

Der Weihnachtsmann wird Geschenke verteilen.

Ο Σάντα πρόκειται να δώσει δώρα.

Santa is going to give out presents.

Der Weihnachtsmann trägt eine Ledertasche mit Geschenken.

Ο Άγιος Βασίλης φέρει μια δερμάτινη τσάντα γεμάτη με δώρα.

Santa Claus is carrying a leather bag filled with gifts.

Name

I Can...

- [ ] read the 1st sentence.
- [ ] read the 2nd sentence.
- [ ] read the 3rd sentence.
- [ ] make my own sentence.
- [ ] color a picture.

Ich habe einen Schneemann gemacht.

Έκανα έναν χιονάνθρωπο.

I made a snowman.

Der Schneemann war gerade mit der Reinigung des Hofes fertig.

Ο χιονάνθρωπος τελείωσε τον καθαρισμό της αυλής.

The snowman was just done cleaning the yard.

Name

I Can...

- [ ] read the 1st sentence.
- [ ] read the 2nd sentence.
- [ ] read the 3rd sentence.
- [ ] make my own sentence.
- [ ] color a picture.

Der Papagei ist bunt.

Ο παπαγάλος είναι πολύχρωμος.

The parrot is colorful.

Der Papagei lernt gerade, wie man am Himmel fliegt.

Ο παπαγάλος απλά μαθαίνει πώς να πετάει στον ουρανό.

The parrot is just learning how to fly in the sky.

Name

I Can...

- [ ] read the 1st sentence.
- [ ] read the 2nd sentence.
- [ ] read the 3rd sentence.
- [ ] make my own sentence.
- [ ] color a picture.

Es gibt viele Tiere.

Υπάρχουν πολλά ζώα.

There are a lot of animals.

Die Tiere haben einen riesigen Schlaf.

Τα ζώα έχουν ένα τεράστιο ύπνο.

The animals are having a giant sleepover.

Name

I Can...

- ☐ read the 1st sentence.
- ☐ read the 2nd sentence.
- ☐ read the 3rd sentence.
- ☐ make my own sentence.
- ☐ color a picture.

Der Mann trägt einen Gürtel.

Ο άντρας φοράει ζώνη.

The man is wearing a belt.

Der Mann kommt, um das Schiff zu reparieren.

Ο άνθρωπος έρχεται να καθορίσει το πλοίο.

The man is coming to fix the ship.

Name

I Can...

- [ ] read the 1st sentence.
- [ ] read the 2nd sentence.
- [ ] read the 3rd sentence.
- [ ] make my own sentence.
- [ ] color a picture.

Das Kaninchen ist sehr jung.

Το κουνέλι είναι πολύ μικρό.

The rabbit is very young.

Der Magier holte ein Kaninchen aus seinem Hut.

Ο μάγος κάλεσε ένα κουνέλι από το καπέλο του.

The magician summoned a rabbit out of his hat.

Name

I Can...

- [ ] read the 1st sentence.
- [ ] read the 2nd sentence.
- [ ] read the 3rd sentence.
- [ ] make my own sentence.
- [ ] color a picture.

Er hat einen Trank.

Έχει ένα φίλτρο.

He has a potion.

Die Frau lernt, Wissenschaftlerin zu werden.

Η γυναίκα μαθαίνει πώς να γίνει επιστήμονας.

The woman is learning how to become a scientist.

Name

I Can...

- [ ] read the 1st sentence.
- [ ] read the 2nd sentence.
- [ ] read the 3rd sentence.
- [ ] make my own sentence.
- [ ] color a picture.

Er trägt eine Sonnenbrille.

Φοράει γυαλιά ηλίου.

He is wearing sunglasses.

Der Polizist ist wütend auf einige faule Teenager.

Ο αστυνομικός είναι θυμωμένος σε κάποιους σάπιους εφήβους.

The policeman is angry at some rotten teenagers.

Name

I Can...

- [ ] read the 1st sentence.
- [ ] read the 2nd sentence.
- [ ] read the 3rd sentence.
- [ ] make my own sentence.
- [ ] color a picture.

Er hat einen Farbeimer.

Έχει ένα κουβά με χρώμα.

He has a bucket of paint.

Der Anstreicher ist fast fertig mit seiner täglichen Arbeit.

Ο ζωγράφος του σπιτιού σχεδόν τελειώνει με την καθημερινή του εργασία.

The house painter is almost done with his daily work.

Name

I Can...

- [ ] read the 1st sentence.
- [ ] read the 2nd sentence.
- [ ] read the 3rd sentence.
- [ ] make my own sentence.
- [ ] color a picture.

Der Mann hat einen Hut.

Ο άνθρωπος έχει ένα καπέλο.

The man has a hat.

Der Postbote liefert im Morgengrauen Post.

Ο ταχυδρόμος στέλνει μηνύματα στη ρωγμή της αυγής.

The postman is delivering mails at the crack of dawn.

Name _______________________ 

I Can...

- [ ] read the 1st sentence.
- [ ] read the 2nd sentence.
- [ ] read the 3rd sentence.
- [ ] make my own sentence.
- [ ] color a picture.

Er hat ein Walkie-Talkie.

Έχει ένα φορητό ραδιοτηλέφωνο.

He has a walkie talkie.

Der Geschäftsmann ruft seinen Chef an.

Ο επιχειρηματίας καλεί τον προϊστάμενό του.

The businessman is calling his boss.

Name

I Can...

- [ ] read the 1st sentence.
- [ ] read the 2nd sentence.
- [ ] read the 3rd sentence.
- [ ] make my own sentence.
- [ ] color a picture.

Er ist schläfrig.

Είναι υπνηλία.

He is sleepy.

Der Arbeiter schleppt einige schwere Kisten.

Ο εργάτης ρυμουλκώνει μερικά βαρύ κουτιά.

The workman is towing some heavy boxes.

Name ___________________ 

I Can...

- [ ] read the 1st sentence.
- [ ] read the 2nd sentence.
- [ ] read the 3rd sentence.
- [ ] make my own sentence.
- [ ] color a picture.

Er trägt eine Fliege.

Φοράει παπιγιόν.

He is wearing a bowtie.

Der Kellner serviert einer Familie frische Limonade.

Ο σερβιτόρος σερβίρει φρέσκια λεμονάδα σε μια οικογένεια.

The waiter is serving fresh lemonade to a family.

Name

I Can...

- [ ] read the 1st sentence.
- [ ] read the 2nd sentence.
- [ ] read the 3rd sentence.
- [ ] make my own sentence.
- [ ] color a picture.

Er hat einen Koffer.

Έχει μια βαλίτσα.

He has a suitcase.

Der Ingenieur wird ein schickes blaues Auto reparieren.

Ο μηχανικός πρόκειται να καθορίσει ένα φανταχτερό μπλε αυτοκίνητο.

The engineer is going to fix a fancy blue car.

Name

I Can...

- [ ] read the 1st sentence.
- [ ] read the 2nd sentence.
- [ ] read the 3rd sentence.
- [ ] make my own sentence.
- [ ] color a picture.

Der Koch hat eine Serviette.

Ο σεφ έχει μια πετσέτα.

The chef has a napkin.

Der Küchenchef machte leckere Pasta für alle zum Teilen.

Ο σεφ έκανε γευστικά ζυμαρικά για να μοιραστούν όλοι.

The chef made yummy pasta for everyone to share.

Name

I Can...

- [ ] read the 1st sentence.
- [ ] read the 2nd sentence.
- [ ] read the 3rd sentence.
- [ ] make my own sentence.
- [ ] color a picture.

Der Hahn hat einen großen Schnabel.

Ο κόκορας έχει ένα μεγάλο ράμφος.

The rooster has a big beak.

Das weiße Huhn trägt einen Künstlerhut.

Το λευκό κοτόπουλο φοράει καπέλο ενός καλλιτέχνη.

The white chicken is wearing an artist's hat.

Name _______________

I Can...

- [ ] read the 1st sentence.
- [ ] read the 2nd sentence.
- [ ] read the 3rd sentence.
- [ ] make my own sentence.
- [ ] color a picture.

Der Vogel ist klein.

Το πουλί είναι μικρό.

The bird is small.

Das kleine Küken spielt mit dem Telefon seiner Mutter Musik.

Η μικρή γκόμενα χρησιμοποιεί το τηλέφωνο της μητέρας του για να παίξει μουσική.

The little chick is using his mother's phone to play music.

Name

I Can...

- [ ] read the 1st sentence.
- [ ] read the 2nd sentence.
- [ ] read the 3rd sentence.
- [ ] make my own sentence.
- [ ] color a picture.

Das ist mein Ring.

Αυτό είναι το δαχτυλίδι μου.

That is my ring.

Auf dem Ring befindet sich ein Diamantjuwel.

Το δαχτυλίδι έχει ένα κόσμημα με διαμάντια πάνω του.

The ring has a diamond jewel on it.

Name ___________________________

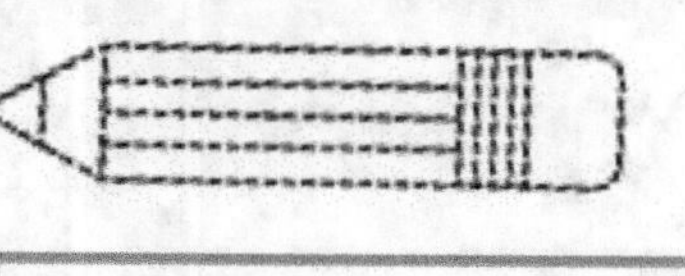

I Can...

- [ ] read the 1st sentence.
- [ ] read the 2nd sentence.
- [ ] read the 3rd sentence.
- [ ] make my own sentence.
- [ ] color a picture.

Die Ente hat drei Eier.

Η πάπια έχει τρία αυγά.

The duck has three eggs.

Die Ente ließ gerade ihre kleinen ovalen Eier fallen.

Η πάπια μόλις έριξε τα μικρά ωοειδή αυγά της.

The duck just dropped its little oval eggs.

Name _______________________ 

I Can...

- [ ] read the 1st sentence.
- [ ] read the 2nd sentence.
- [ ] read the 3rd sentence.
- [ ] make my own sentence.
- [ ] color a picture.

Der Schwan ist wunderschön.

Ο κύκνος είναι όμορφος.

The swan is beautiful.

Der schöne Schwan isst ein Stück grünes Gemüse.

Ο όμορφος κύκνος τρώει ένα κομμάτι πράσινων λαχανικών.

The beautiful swan is eating a piece of green vegetables.

Name ________________

I Can...

- [ ] read the 1st sentence.
- [ ] read the 2nd sentence.
- [ ] read the 3rd sentence.
- [ ] make my own sentence.
- [ ] color a picture.

Das Mädchen trägt ein Kleid.

Το κορίτσι φοράει φόρεμα.

The girl is wearing a dress.

Das kleine Mädchen trägt zwei Eimer voll Wasser.

Το μικρό κορίτσι μεταφέρει δύο κουβάδες φορτία νερού.

The little girl is carrying two buckets loads of water.

Name

I Can...

- [ ] read the 1st sentence.
- [ ] read the 2nd sentence.
- [ ] read the 3rd sentence.
- [ ] make my own sentence.
- [ ] color a picture.

Der Junge rennt.

Το αγόρι τρέχει.

The boy is running.

Der Sprinter gewinnt den ersten Platz in einem Rennen.

Ο σπρίντερ κερδίζει την πρώτη θέση σε έναν αγώνα.

The sprinter is winning first place in a race.

Name ___________________ 

I Can...

- ☐ read the 1st sentence.
- ☐ read the 2nd sentence.
- ☐ read the 3rd sentence.
- ☐ make my own sentence.
- ☐ color a picture.

Er ist ein Musiker.

Είναι μουσικός.

He is a musician.

Der Junge übt die Flöte, um in der Schule fertig zu sein.

Το αγόρι ασκεί το φλάουτο να είναι έτοιμο στο σχολείο.

The boy is practicing the flute to be ready at school.

Name

I Can...

- [ ] read the 1st sentence.
- [ ] read the 2nd sentence.
- [ ] read the 3rd sentence.
- [ ] make my own sentence.
- [ ] color a picture.

Er sieht fröhlich aus.

Φαίνεται χαρούμενος.

He looks joyful.

Der Schlagzeuger leitet eine riesige Kostümparade.

Ο τυμπανιστής οδηγεί μια μεγάλη παρέλαση κοστουμιών.

The drummer is leading a huge costume parade.

Name ______________________

I Can...

- [ ] read the 1st sentence.
- [ ] read the 2nd sentence.
- [ ] read the 3rd sentence.
- [ ] make my own sentence.
- [ ] color a picture.

Der Dinosaurier ist ein Rockstar.

Ο δεινόσαυρος είναι ένα ροκ σταρ.

The dinosaur is a rock star.

Der Traum des Dinosauriers ist es, ein wundervoller Rockstar zu werden.

Το όνειρο του δεινόσαυρου είναι να γίνει ένα υπέροχο ροκ σταρ.

The dinosaur's dream is to become a wonderful rock star.

Name

I Can...

- [ ] read the 1st sentence.
- [ ] read the 2nd sentence.
- [ ] read the 3rd sentence.
- [ ] make my own sentence.
- [ ] color a picture.

Die Krankenschwester hilft dem Arzt.

Η νοσοκόμα βοηθά τον γιατρό.

The nurse helps the doctor.

Die Krankenschwester hilft den Patienten, besser zu werden.

Η νοσοκόμα βοηθά τους ασθενείς να γίνουν καλύτεροι.

The nurse is helping patients get better.

Name ___________________________ 

I Can...

- [ ] read the 1st sentence.
- [ ] read the 2nd sentence.
- [ ] read the 3rd sentence.
- [ ] make my own sentence.
- [ ] color a picture.

Sie trägt eine Krone.

Φοράει στέμμα.

She is wearing a crown.

Der Bienenstock hat einen Anführer, der eine magische Biene ist.

Η κυψέλη έχει έναν ηγέτη ο οποίος είναι μια μαγική μέλισσα.

The beehive has a leader who is a magical bee.

Name _____________

I Can...

- [ ] read the 1st sentence.
- [ ] read the 2nd sentence.
- [ ] read the 3rd sentence.
- [ ] make my own sentence.
- [ ] color a picture.

Es ist orange und schwarz.

Είναι πορτοκαλί και μαύρο.

It is orange and black.

Ein formeller Tiger winkt mit der Hand nach einem gelben Taxi.

Μια επίσημη τίγρη κυματίζει το χέρι του για ένα κίτρινο ταξί.

A formal tiger is waving his hand for a yellow taxi.

Name ___________________________

I Can...

- ☐ read the 1st sentence.
- ☐ read the 2nd sentence.
- ☐ read the 3rd sentence.
- ☐ make my own sentence.
- ☐ color a picture.

Der Junge trägt viele Bücher.

Το αγόρι μεταφέρει πολλά βιβλία.

The boy is carrying a lot of books.

Der kluge kleine Junge trägt schwere Bücher zum Lernen.

Το έξυπνο μικρό αγόρι μεταφέρει βαριά βιβλία για σπουδές.

The smart little boy is carrying heavy books to study.

Name

I Can...

- [ ] read the 1st sentence.
- [ ] read the 2nd sentence.
- [ ] read the 3rd sentence.
- [ ] make my own sentence.
- [ ] color a picture.

Die Pizza sieht köstlich aus.

Η πίτσα φαίνεται υπέροχη.

The pizza looks delicious.

Der Koch nahm gerade den Pizzaofen

Ο σεφ μόλις πήρε το φούρνο πίτσας

The chef just took the pizza oven

Name ___________________________

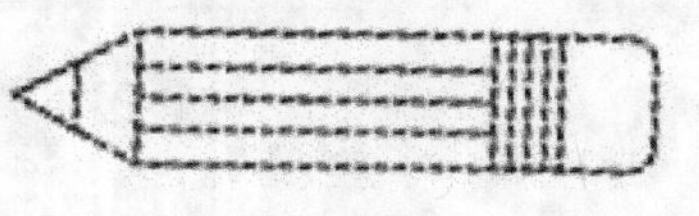

I Can...

- [ ] read the 1st sentence.
- [ ] read the 2nd sentence.
- [ ] read the 3rd sentence.
- [ ] make my own sentence.
- [ ] color a picture.

Das ist der Computer meines Vaters.

Αυτός είναι ο υπολογιστής του μπαμπά μου.

That is my dad's computer.

Der Laptop begrüßt den Benutzer.

Ο φορητός υπολογιστής λέει γεια στον χρήστη.

The laptop is saying hi to the user.

Name _______________________ 

I Can...

- [ ] read the 1st sentence.
- [ ] read the 2nd sentence.
- [ ] read the 3rd sentence.
- [ ] make my own sentence.
- [ ] color a picture.

Der Bauer hat einen Bart.

Ο αγρότης έχει γενειάδα.

The farmer has a beard.

Der Gärtner wird einige Samen pflanzen.

Ο κηπουρός πρόκειται να φυτέψει μερικούς σπόρους.

The gardener is going to plant some seeds.

Name

I Can...

- [ ] read the 1st sentence.
- [ ] read the 2nd sentence.
- [ ] read the 3rd sentence.
- [ ] make my own sentence.
- [ ] color a picture.

Die Erdbeere ist rot.

Η φράουλα είναι κόκκινη.

The strawberry is red.

Die Erdbeere trinkt kalten erfrischenden Saft.

Η φράουλα πίνει κρύο δροσιστικό χυμό.

The strawberry is drinking cold refreshing juice.

Name ______________

I Can...

- [ ] read the 1st sentence.
- [ ] read the 2nd sentence.
- [ ] read the 3rd sentence.
- [ ] make my own sentence.
- [ ] color a picture.

Der Zauberer hat einen Zauberstab.

Ο μάγος έχει μια ραβδί.

The magician has a wand.

Der Zauberer wird einen großen Drachen beschwören.

Ο μάγος θα καλέσει έναν μεγάλο δράκο.

The wizard is going to summon a great big dragon.

Name ___________

I Can...

- ☐ read the 1st sentence.
- ☐ read the 2nd sentence.
- ☐ read the 3rd sentence.
- ☐ make my own sentence.
- ☐ color a picture.

Rentier hat einen Schal.

Ο τάρανδος έχει κασκόλ.

Reindeer has a scarf.

Das Rentier kommt zu spät, um seinen Freunden sein Geschenk zu geben.

Ο τάρανδος καθυστερεί να δώσει το δώρο του στους φίλους του.

The reindeer is late to give his present to his friends.

Name

I Can...

- [ ] read the 1st sentence.
- [ ] read the 2nd sentence.
- [ ] read the 3rd sentence.
- [ ] make my own sentence.
- [ ] color a picture.

Ich habe viele Stifte.

Έχω πολλά μολύβια.

I have a lot of pencils.

Die Schreibgeräte befinden sich in der Blechdose.

Τα εργαλεία γραφής βρίσκονται στο δοχείο κασσίτερου.

The writing utensils are in the tin can.

Name ____________________

I Can...

- [ ] read the 1st sentence.
- [ ] read the 2nd sentence.
- [ ] read the 3rd sentence.
- [ ] make my own sentence.
- [ ] color a picture.

Der Weihnachtsmann ist fett.

Ο Σάντα είναι παχύς.

Santa is fat.

Der Weihnachtsmann lacht über einen lustigen Witz.

Ο Άγιος Βασίλης γελάει σε ένα ξεκαρδιστικό αστείο.

Santa Claus is laughing at a hilarious joke.

Name ___________________ 

I Can...

- [ ] read the 1st sentence.
- [ ] read the 2nd sentence.
- [ ] read the 3rd sentence.
- [ ] make my own sentence.
- [ ] color a picture.

Ich habe eine Nase.

Έχω μύτη.

I have one nose.

Nummer eins belegte bei einem Wettbewerb den ersten Platz.

Ο αριθμός ένα πήρε την πρώτη θέση σε έναν διαγωνισμό.

Number one got first place at a competition.

Name ___________________________

I Can...

- [ ] read the 1st sentence.
- [ ] read the 2nd sentence.
- [ ] read the 3rd sentence.
- [ ] make my own sentence.
- [ ] color a picture.

Ich habe zwei Ohren.

Έχω δύο αυτιά.

I have two ears.

Nummer zwei posiert für ein Selfie.

Ο δεύτερος αριθμός θέτει για μια selfie.

Number two is posing for a selfie.

Name ____________________

I Can...

- [ ] read the 1st sentence.
- [ ] read the 2nd sentence.
- [ ] read the 3rd sentence.
- [ ] make my own sentence.
- [ ] color a picture.

Ich habe drei Knöpfe an meinem Kleid.

Έχω τρία κουμπιά στο φόρεμά μου.

I have three buttons on my dress.

Nummer drei zählt bis drei.

Ο τρίτος αριθμός μετράει σε τρία.

Number three is counting to three.

Name _______________________

I Can...

- ☐ read the 1st sentence.
- ☐ read the 2nd sentence.
- ☐ read the 3rd sentence.
- ☐ make my own sentence.
- ☐ color a picture.

Ich habe 0 Schwänze.

Έχω 0 ουρές.

I have 0 tails.

Die Null sagt gut, indem sie die OK-Geste macht.

Το μηδέν λέει ωραία κάνοντας την εντάξει χειρονομία.

The zero is saying fine by making the okay gesture.

Name 

I Can...

- ☐ read the 1st sentence.
- ☐ read the 2nd sentence.
- ☐ read the 3rd sentence.
- ☐ make my own sentence.
- ☐ color a picture.

Ich habe fünf Finger an einer meiner Hände.

Έχω πέντε δάχτυλα σε 1 από τα χέρια μου.

I have five fingers on 1 of my hands.

Die fünf sagen laut ihren Namen, damit andere es wissen.

Οι πέντε λένε δυνατά το όνομά του, έτσι ώστε να γνωρίζουν και άλλοι.

The five are saying its name out loud, so others will know.

Name

I Can...

- [ ] read the 1st sentence.
- [ ] read the 2nd sentence.
- [ ] read the 3rd sentence.
- [ ] make my own sentence.
- [ ] color a picture.

Meine Katze hat vier Beine.

Η γάτα μου έχει τέσσερα πόδια.

My cat has four legs.

Die vier sahen vier Delfine am Meer.

Οι τέσσερις είδαν τέσσερα δελφίνια στον ωκεανό.

The four saw four dolphins at the ocean.

Name

I Can...

- [ ] read the 1st sentence.
- [ ] read the 2nd sentence.
- [ ] read the 3rd sentence.
- [ ] make my own sentence.
- [ ] color a picture.

Ein Schmetterling hat sechs Beine.

Μια πεταλούδα έχει έξι πόδια.

A butterfly has six legs.

Die sechs springen aufgeregt auf und ab.

Οι έξι είναι ενθουσιασμένοι άλματα πάνω-κάτω.

The six are excitedly jumping up and down.

Name

I Can...

- [ ] read the 1st sentence.
- [ ] read the 2nd sentence.
- [ ] read the 3rd sentence.
- [ ] make my own sentence.
- [ ] color a picture.

Eine Spinne hat acht Beine.

Μια αράχνη έχει οκτώ πόδια.

A spider has eight legs.

Die Acht leckt sich über die Lippen, weil sie acht Tabletts mit gebratenem Hühnchen sieht.

Οι οκτώ γλείφουν το χείλι του επειδή βλέπει οχτώ δίσκους τηγανισμένου κοτόπουλου.

The eight is licking its lip because it sees eight trays of fried chicken.

Name ____________________

I Can...

- [ ] read the 1st sentence.
- [ ] read the 2nd sentence.
- [ ] read the 3rd sentence.
- [ ] make my own sentence.
- [ ] color a picture.

Der Hahn wird die Leute wecken.

Ο κόκορας θα ξυπνήσει τους ανθρώπους.

The rooster is going to wake people up.

Der Hahn weckt alle auf.

Ο κόκορας ξυπνάει όλους.

The rooster is waking up everybody.

Name _______________

I Can...

- [ ] read the 1st sentence.
- [ ] read the 2nd sentence.
- [ ] read the 3rd sentence.
- [ ] make my own sentence.
- [ ] color a picture.

Meine Schwester hat neun Kuscheltiere.

Η αδελφή μου έχει εννέα γεμιστά ζώα.

My sister has nine stuffed animals.

Die Neun sagt, dass $4 + 5 = 9$.

Οι εννέα λένε ότι $4 + 5 = 9$.

The nine is saying that $4+5=9$.

Name _______________________ 

I Can...

- [ ] read the 1st sentence.
- [ ] read the 2nd sentence.
- [ ] read the 3rd sentence.
- [ ] make my own sentence.
- [ ] color a picture.

Das Bienenbaby hat gelbe und schwarze Streifen.

Η μέλισσα του μωρού έχει κίτρινες και μαύρες ρίγες.

The baby bee has yellow and black stripes.

Die Babybienen haben sehr kleine Flügel.

Οι μέλισσες έχουν πολύ μικροσκοπικά φτερά.

The baby bees have very tiny wings.

Name

I Can...

- [ ] read the 1st sentence.
- [ ] read the 2nd sentence.
- [ ] read the 3rd sentence.
- [ ] make my own sentence.
- [ ] color a picture.

Der Marienkäfer hat viele Stellen.

Η πασχαλίτσα έχει πολλά σημεία.

The ladybug has many spots.

Der Marienkäfer isst ein Stück Salat.

Η πασχαλίτσα τρώει ένα κομμάτι μαρούλι.

The ladybug is eating a piece of lettuce.

Name

I Can...

- [ ] read the 1st sentence.
- [ ] read the 2nd sentence.
- [ ] read the 3rd sentence.
- [ ] make my own sentence.
- [ ] color a picture.

Die Schafe sind dünn.

Τα πρόβατα είναι κοκαλιάρα.

The sheep are skinny.

Dieses Schaf ist so flauschig.

Αυτό το πρόβατο είναι τόσο αφράτο.

This sheep is so fluffy.

Name

I Can...

- [ ] read the 1st sentence.
- [ ] read the 2nd sentence.
- [ ] read the 3rd sentence.
- [ ] make my own sentence.
- [ ] color a picture.

Der Hase nimmt an einem Eiermalwettbewerb teil.

Το κουνέλι μπαίνει σε διαγωνισμό ζωγραφικής αυγών.

The rabbit is entering an egg painting contest.

Der Osterhase malt gerne Eier.

Το Πάσχα Μπάνι αρέσει να ζωγραφίζει τα αυγά.

The Easter Bunny likes to paint eggs.

Name

I Can...

- [ ] read the 1st sentence.
- [ ] read the 2nd sentence.
- [ ] read the 3rd sentence.
- [ ] make my own sentence.
- [ ] color a picture.

Die Eule ist Sprachlehrerin.

Η κουκουβάγια είναι καθηγητής γλωσσών.

The owl is a language arts teacher.

Mr.Owl unterrichtet die 3. Klasse.

Ο κ. Owl διδάσκει την 3η τάξη.

Mr.Owl teaches the 3rd grade.

Name

I Can...

- [ ] read the 1st sentence.
- [ ] read the 2nd sentence.
- [ ] read the 3rd sentence.
- [ ] make my own sentence.
- [ ] color a picture.

Der Mann hat einen alten Hammer.

Ο άνθρωπος έχει ένα αρχαίο σφυρί.

The man has an ancient hammer.

Der Mann hat einen glänzenden neuen Hammer gekauft.

Ο άνθρωπος έχει αγοράσει ένα λαμπερό νέο σφυρί.

The man has bought a shiny new hammer.

Name

I Can...

- ☐ read the 1st sentence.
- ☐ read the 2nd sentence.
- ☐ read the 3rd sentence.
- ☐ make my own sentence.
- ☐ color a picture.

Die Ziege hat einen Freund.

Η κατσίκα έχει φίλο.

The goat has a friend.

Die Ziege hat vier Hufe.

Η κατσίκα έχει τέσσερις οπλές.

The goat has four hooves.

Name

I Can...

- [ ] read the 1st sentence.
- [ ] read the 2nd sentence.
- [ ] read the 3rd sentence.
- [ ] make my own sentence.
- [ ] color a picture.

Die Freundin meiner Mutter ist eine Magd.

Ο φίλος της μαμάς μου είναι κοπέλα.

My mom's friend is a maid.

Die Magd hat einen großen braunen Besen.

Η κοπέλα έχει μια μεγάλη καφέ σκούπα.

The maid has a big brown broom.

Name

I Can...

- [ ] read the 1st sentence.
- [ ] read the 2nd sentence.
- [ ] read the 3rd sentence.
- [ ] make my own sentence.
- [ ] color a picture.

Ich bin in den Zoo gegangen.

Πήγα στο ζωολογικό κήπο.

I went to the zoo.

Die Tiere luden den Affen und den Papagei zum Übernachten ein.

Τα ζώα κάλεσαν τον πίθηκο και τον παπαγάλο να ενταχθούν στον ύπνο τους.

The animals invited the monkey and the parrot to join their sleepover.

Name

I Can...

- [ ] read the 1st sentence.
- [ ] read the 2nd sentence.
- [ ] read the 3rd sentence.
- [ ] make my own sentence.
- [ ] color a picture.

Der Dinosaurier hat ein Kissen.

Ο δεινόσαυρος έχει ένα μαξιλάρι.

The dinosaur has a pillow.

Der Dinosaurier bekommt einen Teller für sein Essen.

Ο δεινόσαυρος παίρνει ένα πιάτο για το φαγητό του.

The dinosaur is getting a plate for his food.

Name ______________________ 

I Can...

- [ ] read the 1st sentence.
- [ ] read the 2nd sentence.
- [ ] read the 3rd sentence.
- [ ] make my own sentence.
- [ ] color a picture.

Der Junge freut sich auf den Schulbesuch.

Το αγόρι είναι ενθουσιασμένο για να πάει στο σχολείο.

The boy is excited to go to school.

Der Junge bereitet sich auf die Schule vor.

Το αγόρι ετοιμάζεται για το σχολείο.

The boy is preparing for school.

Name _______________________

I Can...

- [ ] read the 1st sentence.
- [ ] read the 2nd sentence.
- [ ] read the 3rd sentence.
- [ ] make my own sentence.
- [ ] color a picture.

Die Kinder im Schulbus gehen zur Schule.

Τα παιδιά στο σχολικό λεωφορείο πηγαίνουν στο σχολείο.

The kids on the school bus are going to school.

Die Kinder gehen in einem Bus zur Schule.

Τα παιδιά πηγαίνουν στο σχολείο με λεωφορείο.

The children go to school on a bus.

Name 

I Can...

- ☐ read the 1st sentence.
- ☐ read the 2nd sentence.
- ☐ read the 3rd sentence.
- ☐ make my own sentence.
- ☐ color a picture.

Die Kobra ist sehr schön.

Η κόμπρα είναι πολύ όμορφη.

The cobra is very lovely.

Die Anakonda ist die längste Schlange der Welt.

Το anaconda είναι το μακρύτερο φίδι στον κόσμο.

The anaconda is the longest snake in the world.

Name _______________________ 

I Can...

- [ ] read the 1st sentence.
- [ ] read the 2nd sentence.
- [ ] read the 3rd sentence.
- [ ] make my own sentence.
- [ ] color a picture.

Das ist ein fetter Hund!

Αυτό είναι ένα λιπαρό σκυλί!

That is a fat dog!

Der Hund hat ein goldenes Halsband.

Ο σκύλος έχει ένα χρυσό κολάρο.

The dog has a golden collar.

Name

I Can...

- [ ] read the 1st sentence.
- [ ] read the 2nd sentence.
- [ ] read the 3rd sentence.
- [ ] make my own sentence.
- [ ] color a picture.

Der Elefant lebt im Zoo.

Ο ελέφαντας ζει στον ζωολογικό κήπο.

The elephant lives in the zoo.

Der Elefant hat einen langen Stamm.

Ο ελέφαντας έχει ένα μακρύ κορμό.

The elephant has a long trunk.

Name ____________________

I Can...

- [ ] read the 1st sentence.
- [ ] read the 2nd sentence.
- [ ] read the 3rd sentence.
- [ ] make my own sentence.
- [ ] color a picture.

Die Giraffe isst Gemüse.

Η καμηλοπάρδαλη τρώει λαχανικά.

The giraffe eats vegetables.

Die Giraffe hat viele Stellen.

Η καμηλοπάρδαλη έχει πολλά σημεία.

The giraffe has many spots.

Name

I Can...

- [ ] read the 1st sentence.
- [ ] read the 2nd sentence.
- [ ] read the 3rd sentence.
- [ ] make my own sentence.
- [ ] color a picture.

Der Chipmunk hat einen weichen Bauch.

Το chipmunk έχει μια μαλακή κοιλιά.

The chipmunk has a soft tummy.

Der Streifenhörnchen brachte eine riesige Eichel nach Hause.

Ο chipmunk έφερε στο σπίτι ένα γιγάντιο βελανίδι.

The chipmunk brought home a giant acorn.

Name ______________________

I Can...

- [ ] read the 1st sentence.
- [ ] read the 2nd sentence.
- [ ] read the 3rd sentence.
- [ ] make my own sentence.
- [ ] color a picture.

Ich habe insgesamt zehn Zehen.

Έχω δέκα δάχτυλα συνολικά.

I have ten toes in total.

Eins und Null zusammen sind zehn.

Ο ένας και ο μηδέν μαζί είναι δέκα.

One and Zero together are ten.

Name

I Can...

- [ ] read the 1st sentence.
- [ ] read the 2nd sentence.
- [ ] read the 3rd sentence.
- [ ] make my own sentence.
- [ ] color a picture.

Der Alligator springt.

Ο αλλιγάτορας είναι άλμα.

The alligator is jumping.

Das springende Krokodil ist glücklich.

Ο κροκόδειλος άλματος είναι ευτυχισμένος.

The jumping crocodile is happy.

Name

I Can...

- [ ] read the 1st sentence.
- [ ] read the 2nd sentence.
- [ ] read the 3rd sentence.
- [ ] make my own sentence.
- [ ] color a picture.

Ich habe eine Ameise gefunden.

Βρήκα ένα μυρμήγκι.

I found an ant.

Eine Ameise ist klein, aber sehr stark.

Ένα μυρμήγκι είναι μικρό μέγεθος, αλλά πολύ ισχυρό.

An ant is tiny in size, but very strong.

Name

I Can...

- ☐ read the 1st sentence.
- ☐ read the 2nd sentence.
- ☐ read the 3rd sentence.
- ☐ make my own sentence.
- ☐ color a picture.

Die Fledermaus schläft verkehrt herum.

Το ρόπαλο κοιμάται ανάποδα.

The bat sleeps upside down.

Die Fledermaus umarmt den Brief.

Το ρόπαλο αγκαλιάζει το γράμμα.

The bat is hugging the letter.

Name ___________________________

I Can...

- [ ] read the 1st sentence.
- [ ] read the 2nd sentence.
- [ ] read the 3rd sentence.
- [ ] make my own sentence.
- [ ] color a picture.

Die Katze ist sehr müde.

Η γάτα είναι πολύ κουρασμένη.

The cat is very tired.

Die Katze ist sehr müde.

Η γάτα είναι πολύ υπνηλία.

The cat is very sleepy.

Name

I Can...

- ☐ read the 1st sentence.
- ☐ read the 2nd sentence.
- ☐ read the 3rd sentence.
- ☐ make my own sentence.
- ☐ color a picture.

Der Hund spielt gern.

Το σκυλί αρέσει να παίζει.

The dog likes to play.

Der Hund leckt gerne den Knochen.

Το σκυλί αρέσει να γλείφει το κόκκαλο.

The dog likes to lick the bone.

Name

Der Elefant hat Wimpern.

Ο ελέφαντας έχει βλεφαρίδες.

The elephant has eyelashes.

Der Elefant hat große Ohren.

Ο ελέφαντας έχει μεγάλα αυτιά.

The elephant has big ears.

Name

I Can...

- ☐ read the 1st sentence.
- ☐ read the 2nd sentence.
- ☐ read the 3rd sentence.
- ☐ make my own sentence.
- ☐ color a picture.

Der Frosch hüpft.

Ο βάτραχος αναπηδά.

The frog is hopping.

Der Frosch nutzt seine Zunge, um Beute zu fangen.

Ο βάτραχος χρησιμοποιεί τη γλώσσα του για να πιάσει λεία.

The frog uses its tongue to catch prey.

Name

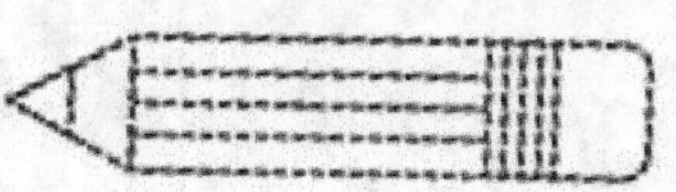

I Can...

- ☐ read the 1st sentence.
- ☐ read the 2nd sentence.
- ☐ read the 3rd sentence.
- ☐ make my own sentence.
- ☐ color a picture.

Die Ziege läuft müde herum.

Η κατσίκα περπατάει ύπνο.

The goat is sleepily walking around.

Die Ziege weidet auf der Wiese.

Η κατσίκα βόσκουν στο λιβάδι.

The goat is grazing in the meadow.

Name

I Can...

- [ ] read the 1st sentence.
- [ ] read the 2nd sentence.
- [ ] read the 3rd sentence.
- [ ] make my own sentence.
- [ ] color a picture.

Das Nilpferd hat einen großen Kopf.

Ο ιππότης έχει ένα μεγάλο κεφάλι.

The hippo has a big head.

Das Nilpferd ist erstaunt, wie groß seine Zähne sind.

Ο ιππότης είναι έκπληκτος για το πόσο μεγάλα είναι τα δόντια του.

The hippo is amazed at how big his teeth are.

Name ___________________

I Can...

- [ ] read the 1st sentence.
- [ ] read the 2nd sentence.
- [ ] read the 3rd sentence.
- [ ] make my own sentence.
- [ ] color a picture.

Der Leguan hat einen langen Schwanz.

Η ιγκουάνα έχει μακρά ουρά.

The iguana has a long tail.

Der Leguan kräuselt sich um das Alphabet.

Η ιγκουάνα περιστρέφεται γύρω από το αλφάβητο.

The iguana is curling around the alphabet.

Name ______________________

I Can...

- [ ] read the 1st sentence.
- [ ] read the 2nd sentence.
- [ ] read the 3rd sentence.
- [ ] make my own sentence.
- [ ] color a picture.

Mama kaufte eine neue Flasche Marmelade.

Το μαμά αγόρασε ένα νέο μπουκάλι μαρμελάδας.

Mom bought a new bottle of jam.

Sie können Marmelade auf Toast geben, um ihm mehr Geschmack zu verleihen.

Μπορείτε να βάλετε μαρμελάδα στο τοστ για να το δώσετε μεγαλύτερη γεύση.

You can put jam on toast to give it more taste.

Name _______________________ 

I Can...

- [ ] read the 1st sentence.
- [ ] read the 2nd sentence.
- [ ] read the 3rd sentence.
- [ ] make my own sentence.
- [ ] color a picture.

Der Drachen hat einen schönen Schwanz.

Ο χαρταετός έχει μια όμορφη ουρά.

The kite has a beautiful tail.

Der Drachen ist am Boden.

Ο χαρταετός είναι στο έδαφος.

The kite is on the ground.

Name

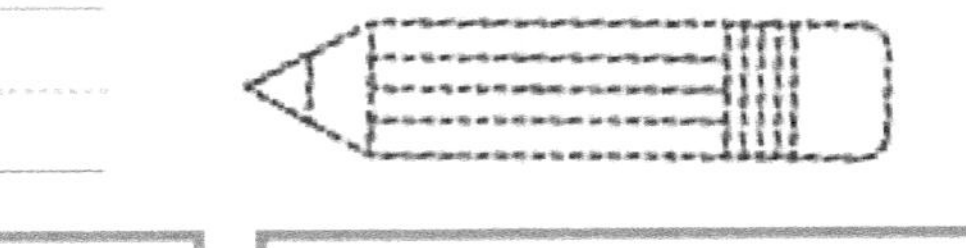

I Can...

- ☐ read the 1st sentence.
- ☐ read the 2nd sentence.
- ☐ read the 3rd sentence.
- ☐ make my own sentence.
- ☐ color a picture.

Der Löwe ist schüchtern.

Το λιοντάρι είναι δειλά.

The lion is timid.

Der Löwe jagt seinen Schwanz.

Το λιοντάρι κυνηγάει την ουρά του.

The lion is chasing its tail.

Name ___________________

I Can...

- ☐ read the 1st sentence.
- ☐ read the 2nd sentence.
- ☐ read the 3rd sentence.
- ☐ make my own sentence.
- ☐ color a picture.

Ich mag Mäuse.

Μου αρέσουν τα ποντίκια.

I like mice.

Die Maus hat sehr lange Schnurrhaare.

Το ποντίκι έχει πολύ μακρύ μουστάκι.

The mouse has very long whiskers.

Name

I Can...

- [ ] read the 1st sentence.
- [ ] read the 2nd sentence.
- [ ] read the 3rd sentence.
- [ ] make my own sentence.
- [ ] color a picture.

Die Nase atmet.

Η μύτη αναπνέει.

The nose is breathing.

Die Nase dient zum Riechen von Dingen.

Η μύτη χρησιμοποιείται για τη μυρωδιά των πραγμάτων.

The nose is used for smelling things.

Name

I Can...

- [ ] read the 1st sentence.
- [ ] read the 2nd sentence.
- [ ] read the 3rd sentence.
- [ ] make my own sentence.
- [ ] color a picture.

Der Oktopus lebt unter Wasser.

Το χταπόδι ζει υποβρύχια.

The octopus lives underwater.

Die Krake hat sehr lange Tentakeln.

Το χταπόδι έχει πολύ μακρά πλοκάμια.

The octopus has very long tentacles.

Name _______________

I Can...

- [ ] read the 1st sentence.
- [ ] read the 2nd sentence.
- [ ] read the 3rd sentence.
- [ ] make my own sentence.
- [ ] color a picture.

Der Pinguin frisst Fisch.

Ο πιγκουίνος τρώει ψάρι.

The penguin eats fish.

Der Pinguin lebt in kalten Regionen.

Ο πιγκουίνος ζει σε κρύες περιοχές.

The penguin lives in cold regions.

Name ___________________

I Can...

- [ ] read the 1st sentence.
- [ ] read the 2nd sentence.
- [ ] read the 3rd sentence.
- [ ] make my own sentence.
- [ ] color a picture.

Die Königin hat einen Zauberstab.

Η βασίλισσα έχει μια ραβδί.

The queen has a wand.

Die Königin hat einen rosa Zauberstab.

Η βασίλισσα έχει ροζ ραβδί.

The queen has a pink wand.

Name ____________________

I Can...

- [ ] read the 1st sentence.
- [ ] read the 2nd sentence.
- [ ] read the 3rd sentence.
- [ ] make my own sentence.
- [ ] color a picture.

Der Hase hat lange Ohren.

Το κουνέλι έχει μακρά αυτιά.

The rabbit has long ears.

Der Hase ist verwirrt.

Το κουνέλι είναι συγκεχυμένο.

The rabbit is confused.

Name

I Can...

- [ ] read the 1st sentence.
- [ ] read the 2nd sentence.
- [ ] read the 3rd sentence.
- [ ] make my own sentence.
- [ ] color a picture.

Die Schlange hat Tupfen.

Το φίδι έχει πολικές τελείες.

The snake has polka dots.

Die Schlange ist sehr schleimig.

Το φίδι είναι πολύ γλοιώδες.

The snake is very slimy.

Name

I Can...

- ☐ read the 1st sentence.
- ☐ read the 2nd sentence.
- ☐ read the 3rd sentence.
- ☐ make my own sentence.
- ☐ color a picture.

Die Schildkröte hat eine spitze Schale.

Η χελώνα έχει ένα μυτερό κέλυφος.

The tortoise has a pointy shell.

Die Schildkröte lebt an Land, im Gegensatz zu Schildkröten.

Η χελώνα ζει στη γη, σε αντίθεση με τις χελώνες.

The tortoise lives on land, unlike turtles.

Name

I Can...

- [ ] read the 1st sentence.
- [ ] read the 2nd sentence.
- [ ] read the 3rd sentence.
- [ ] make my own sentence.
- [ ] color a picture.

Es regnet.

Βρέχει.

It's raining.

Der Regenschirm schützt dich.

Η ομπρέλα σας προστατεύει.

The umbrella shelters you.

Name

I Can...

- [ ] read the 1st sentence.
- [ ] read the 2nd sentence.
- [ ] read the 3rd sentence.
- [ ] make my own sentence.
- [ ] color a picture.

Die Geige ist ein Musikinstrument.

Το βιολί είναι ένα μουσικό όργανο.

The violin is a musical instrument.

Die Geige ist eines der fantastischsten Instrumente.

Το βιολί είναι ένα από τα πιο φανταστικά όργανα.

The violin is one of the most fantastic instruments.

Name

I Can...

- [ ] read the 1st sentence.
- [ ] read the 2nd sentence.
- [ ] read the 3rd sentence.
- [ ] make my own sentence.
- [ ] color a picture.

Das Walross hat einen Freund.

Ο θάλαμος έχει φίλο.

The walrus has a friend.

Das Walross hat einen Schwanz.

Ο θάλαμος έχει μια ουρά.

The walrus has a tail.

Name

I Can...

- [ ] read the 1st sentence.
- [ ] read the 2nd sentence.
- [ ] read the 3rd sentence.
- [ ] make my own sentence.
- [ ] color a picture.

Das Xylophon ist ein buntes Instrument.

Το ξυλόφωνο είναι ένα πολύχρωμο όργανο.

The xylophone is a colorful instrument.

Das Xylophon ist ein sehr cooles Instrument.

Το ξυλόφωνο είναι ένα πολύ δροσερό όργανο.

The xylophone is a very cool instrument.

Name _______________________

I Can...

- [ ] read the 1st sentence.
- [ ] read the 2nd sentence.
- [ ] read the 3rd sentence.
- [ ] make my own sentence.
- [ ] color a picture.

Der Junge hat einen kleinen Hut.

Το αγόρι έχει ένα μικρό καπέλο.

The boy has a little hat.

Das Kind hat ein sehr buntes Jojo.

Το παιδί έχει ένα πολύχρωμο yoyo.

The kid has a very colorful yoyo.

Name

I Can...

- [ ] read the 1st sentence.
- [ ] read the 2nd sentence.
- [ ] read the 3rd sentence.
- [ ] make my own sentence.
- [ ] color a picture.

Das Zebra hat einen Schwanz.

Η ζέβρα έχει μια ουρά.

The zebra has a tail.

Das Zebra lächelt weit

Η ζέβρα χαμογελάει ευρέως

The zebra is smiling widely

Name

I Can...

- [ ] read the 1st sentence.
- [ ] read the 2nd sentence.
- [ ] read the 3rd sentence.
- [ ] make my own sentence.
- [ ] color a picture.

Ich habe eine Kerze auf meinem Kuchen.

Έχω ένα κερί στο κέικ μου.

I have a candle on my cake.

Diese Geburtstagstorte ist für ein kleines Kind.

Αυτή η τούρτα γενεθλίων είναι για ένα μικρό παιδί.

This birthday cake is for a little kids.

Name

I Can...

- [ ] read the 1st sentence.
- [ ] read the 2nd sentence.
- [ ] read the 3rd sentence.
- [ ] make my own sentence.
- [ ] color a picture.

Der Astronaut ist auf Mission.

Ο αστροναύτης πηγαίνει σε μια αποστολή.

The astronaut is going on a mission.

Der Astronaut sah etwas in der Ferne.

Ο αστροναύτης είδε κάτι σε απόσταση.

The astronaut saw something in the distance.

Name

I Can...

- [ ] read the 1st sentence.
- [ ] read the 2nd sentence.
- [ ] read the 3rd sentence.
- [ ] make my own sentence.
- [ ] color a picture.

Der Samurai geht morgens joggen.

Ο σαμουράι πηγαίνει για πρωινή jog.

The samurai is going for a morning jog.

Der Samurai jagt seinen Feind weg.

Ο σαμουράι κυνηγάει τον εχθρό του.

The samurai is chasing away his enemy.

Name ______________________

I Can...

- [ ] read the 1st sentence.
- [ ] read the 2nd sentence.
- [ ] read the 3rd sentence.
- [ ] make my own sentence.
- [ ] color a picture.

Mein Freund hat einen riesigen Kuchen.

Ο φίλος μου έχει μια γιγαντιαία τούρτα.

My friend is having a gigantic cake.

Diese Geburtstagstorte hat drei Schichten.

Αυτή η τούρτα γενεθλίων έχει τρία στρώματα.

This birthday cake has three layers.

Name

I Can...

- [ ] read the 1st sentence.
- [ ] read the 2nd sentence.
- [ ] read the 3rd sentence.
- [ ] make my own sentence.
- [ ] color a picture.

Der Frosch jagt die Fliege.

Ο βάτραχος κυνηγάει τη μύγα.

The frog is chasing the fly.

Der Frosch fängt eine Fliege.

Ο βάτραχος τραβάει μια μύγα.

The frog is catching a fly.

Name

I Can...

- [ ] read the 1st sentence.
- [ ] read the 2nd sentence.
- [ ] read the 3rd sentence.
- [ ] make my own sentence.
- [ ] color a picture.

Der Marienkäfer hat sechs Beine.

Η πασχαλίτσα έχει έξι πόδια.

The ladybug has six legs.

Der Marienkäfer lächelt.

Η πασχαλίτσα χαμογελάει.

The ladybug is smiling.

Name __________________________ 

I Can...

- [ ] read the 1st sentence.
- [ ] read the 2nd sentence.
- [ ] read the 3rd sentence.
- [ ] make my own sentence.
- [ ] color a picture.

Der Drache ist krank.

Ο δράκος είναι άρρωστος.

The dragon is sick.

Der Drache ist sehr durstig.

Ο δράκος είναι πολύ διψασμένος.

The dragon is very thirsty.

Name

I Can...

- [ ] read the 1st sentence.
- [ ] read the 2nd sentence.
- [ ] read the 3rd sentence.
- [ ] make my own sentence.
- [ ] color a picture.

Das ist eine kleine Kuh.

Αυτή είναι μια αγελάδα.

That is a baby cow.

Das Kalb irrt herum.

Ο μόσχος περιπλανιέται.

The calf is wandering around.